Trails of Wonder

TRAILS OF WONDER

Writings on Nature and Man
by John Muir,
Founder of the Sierra Club

Edited by Peter Seymour
Photographs by Richard Fanolio

Hallmark Editions

Excerpts from John of the Mountains: *The Unpublished Journals of John Muir,* edited by Linnie Marsh Wolfe. Copyright 1938 by Wanda Muir Hanna, renewed 1966 by John Muir Hanna and Ralph Eugene Wolfe. "The Earthquake" from Our National Parks. Copyright, 1901, by John Muir. "John Muir, Conservationist" by Edwin Way Teale from The Wilderness World of John Muir. Copyright 1954 by Edwin Way Teale. "Bees" and "Survival" from Steep Trails by John Muir, edited by William Frederic Bade. Copyright 1918 by Houghton Mifflin Company, renewed 1946 by Helen Muir Funk. Reprinted by arrangement with Houghton Mifflin Company.

The Life of John Muir
by Edwin Way Teale

There is, in Muir's published journals, *John of the Mountains,* a moving photograph of the author as an old man peering up at the Sierra cliffs he had scaled in his prime. But always, even in his most daring undertakings, there was a goal of importance. He was never merely seeking thrills or going afield for trophies. To understand Muir and the fire that burned in him, it is necessary to realize that for him all outdoors was at once a laboratory for research and a temple for worship.

All of his early journals were set down with no thought of publication. He shaped his books from his notes more to entice people to look at nature's loveliness than from the pleasure writing gave him. Muir talked easily, fluently. But he wrote laboriously, rewriting, polishing, complaining that it took him a month to write a chapter that could be read in an hour. While laboring with his pen in San Francisco, he wrote to his sister Sarah: "My life these days is like the life of a glacier, one eternal grind, and the top of my head suffers a weariness at times that you know nothing about." Moreover he disliked the solitary confinement of authorship. He was always delighted to see a friend arrive so he could drop writing for a good talk. He never used a typewriter. In his earlier years he cut his own quill pens, sometimes from eagle feathers he found among the mountains. His handwriting grew progressively worse, until at last it was almost as illegible as Thoreau's. His final work was done in a cluttered upstairs study at the ranch house at Martinez, California, where he lived alone with a taciturn Chinese employee who could speak hardly thirty words of English after three decades in America, and who invariably replied when Muir asked him if he understood directions he had given him, "Too muchee talk!"

Before his first book came from the press John Muir was already famous as a writer. His sequence of "Sierra Stud-

ies" in the old *Overland Month-*
ly and his articles in the *Cen-*
tury Magazine...had given
him a national reputation. In
the 1880's and early 1890's,
the present tidal wave of printed matter was only a ripple
and leading periodicals had a permanence and standing
unknown today. Subscribers read them carefully from first
page to last. It was among such readers that Muir was first
recognized as a writer of importance. An exactness and
depth of firsthand observation characterizes all his pages.
He was by turn a scientist, a poet, a mystic, a philosopher,
a humorist. Because he saw everything, mountains and
streams and landscapes, as evolving, unfinished, in the
process of creation, there is a pervading sense of vitality
in all he wrote.

Twice Muir had prospects of making a large fortune. Both
times he turned aside from the path to wealth to return to
these glories of nature. In the library of the Wisconsin
Historical Society, at Madison, I once examined charts
John Muir had made to increase the efficiency of the wag-
on-wheel factory at Indianapolis, Indiana, where he worked
in 1866 and 1867. Had he continued to devote his inven-
tive and administrative abilities to factory work, there is
no doubt he would have become an extremely wealthy
man. A sharp-pointed file that slipped early in March
1867 and pierced the edge of the cornea of his right eye

turned him forever away from machines and back to nature. As he lay in a darkened room during convalescence, shut away from all the beauties of the out-of-doors, he resolved to waste no more of his years in indoor work. Almost as soon as his sight was restored, he set out on his thousand-mile walk to the Gulf.

Again, after his marriage to Louie Wanda Strenzel of Martinez, California, in 1880, Muir rented land from his father-in-law in the alluvial Alhambra Valley and concentrated on raising Tokay grapes, Bartlett pears and other fruit. By devising special equipment for setting out orchard trees, by care in packing, by developing new markets for his fruit, by sharp management and Scotch thrift, he cleared $10,000 a year for ten years. It was his habit to visit the Martinez bank carrying his deposits and valuable papers in a white sack conspicuously marked "Laundry." Other ranchers in the region soon discovered they had to get up early in the morning, literally, to keep ahead of Muir. The wooden lug-boxes in which the fruit was shipped to San Francisco were returned empty to a nearby railroad station on a train that arrived around midnight. They were unmarked but each rancher knew the number that belonged to him. Muir used to get up in the middle of the night to be first on hand. He took exactly his number of boxes but he always picked the perfect, undamaged ones. An innovator in everything he did, John Muir was the first to ship grapes from California to Hawaii. At the end of ten years he told his long-time friend William E. Colby that he had cleared  $100,000 and had all the wealth he would ever want. He turned his back once more on moneymaking. During the Harriman Expedition to Alaska in 1899, someone mentioned the great wealth of the sponsor, the railroad magnate, E. H. Harriman. Muir replied, "Why, I am richer than Harriman. I have all the money I want and he hasn't."

All he needed to do to get ready for an expedition, Muir said, was to "throw some tea and bread in an old sack and jump over the back fence." He preferred bread with a thick crust and always dried it thoroughly to prevent molding. It was his habit occasionally to let his breadsack roll downhill before him, thus producing the fragments which, with a cup of tea, formed his frugal meals. While in the wilderness, he declared, he lived on "essences and crumbs" and his pack was as "unsubstantial as a squirrel's tail."

He never carried a gun. Traveling alone and far from any other human being for weeks at a time, he never was harmed by bear or rattlesnake, never was seriously injured in an accident. Eliphaz the Temanite might well have addressed to Muir his words: "...thou shalt be in league with the stones of the field; and the beasts of the

field will be at peace with thee." In this world where men are afraid they will catch cold, afraid they will lose their way, afraid they will be eaten by bears or bitten by snakes or touch poison ivy or fall over a log, John Muir, faring forth into the wilderness unarmed and alone, was the man unafraid. He was unafraid of danger, of hardship, of wildness, of being alone, of facing death. He was unafraid of public opinion. He was unafraid of work and poverty and hunger. He knew them all and he remained unafraid.

Considerable as was John Muir's contribution to science, even greater was his stature in the long fight for conservation. During those critical years around the turn of the century, his was the most eloquent and powerful voice raised in defense of nature. He was the spearhead of the western movement to preserve wild beauty, a prime mover in the national park system so valued today. Beside a campfire at Soda Springs on the Tuolumne Meadows in 1889, he and Robert Underwood Johnson mapped the seventeen-year battle that preserved Yosemite as a national park. Beside other campfires under sequoias, while on a three-day outing with Theodore Roosevelt in 1903, he presented the case for the preservation of numerous wilderness areas with moving effect. Major credit for saving the Grand Canyon and the Petrified Forest, in Arizona, is ascribed to John Muir. He was president of the Sierra Club from the formation of that militant conservation organization in 1892 until the  time of his death in 1914. His last long battle to save Hetch Hetchy, the beautiful Yosemite Park valley flooded to form a reservoir for San Francisco water — water that could have been obtained elsewhere — ended only the year before he died. It represents one of the great heroic struggles of conservation, no less heroic because the cause was lost.

Near the end of his life Muir said to a close friend, "I have lived a bully life. I have done what I set out to do." Rich in time, rich in enjoyment, rich in appreciation, rich in enthusiasm, rich in understanding, rich in expression, rich in friends, rich in knowledge, John Muir lived a full and rounded life, a life unique in many ways, admirable in many ways, valuable in many ways. "A man in his books," he once wrote, "may be said to walk the earth long after he had gone." In his writings and in his conservation achievements, Muir seems especially present in a world that is better because he lived here. His finest monument is the wild beauty he called attention to and helped preserve — beauty, however, that is never entirely safe, beauty that needs as vigilant protection today and tomorrow as it needed yesterday.

TRAILS OF WONDER

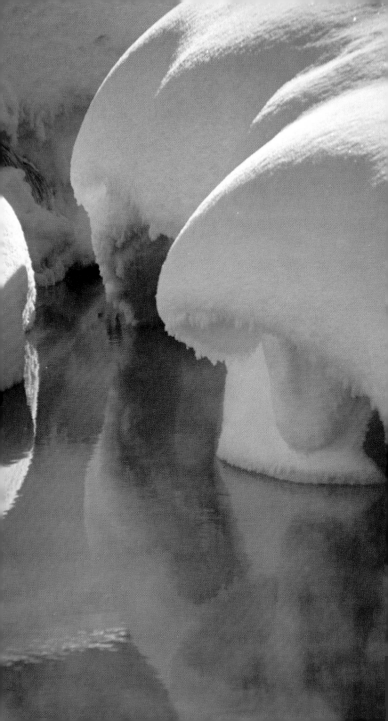

After Snow

The storm past, every feature of the valley is shining in new beauty. Every rock and tree and stump, leafy or leafless, is blooming in glorious snow flowers. No mountain rock of the walls wears snow robes with so queenly a mien as Tissiack. She looks alive, sublime in every feature. The massed sublimity of snow jewels laid on every pine and bush and carved tablet and niche brings them forward. Snow avalanches from rocks continue all day, with noise and appearance of waterfalls bursting into existence and fading suddenly, like meteors. Also the constant thuds from heavy-laden pines, of snow avalanches or cascades, disturbed by a wind breath or sun gleam. The topmost accumulations on tall pines are frequently set free, and as they pour through the other lower branches jostle their white fur also, and thus frequently the whole snow-laden spire is enveloped in a cascade of dusty broken snow. A sudden breeze on the breaking up of a storm will dislodge vast quantities of heaped-up snow, from oak and pine groves at once, filling the air as with a cloud. Many unsound branches are thus removed and Nature's orchards pruned. The live oak collects a smoother crown of snow and wears it longer than any other tree. The black oak has a beautiful appearance — black trunks and limbs laden with intensely white unshaded snow.... Pines have dark caverns beneath the whorls of snow-bent aggregated branches; so also has the Libocedrus, but these are not so dark. Fine bland, cloudless shine all day. Tree and rock shadows on smooth bossy snow sheets.... This evening, the valley is filled with pale, half-transparent frozen vapor....The banks of the river are nobly rounded and shaded. I place cans for birds in feeding places....

Wind

How far it has come, and how far it has to go! How many faces it has fanned, singing, skimming the levels of the sea; floating, sustaining the wide-winged gulls and albatrosses; searching the intricacies of the woods, taking up and carrying their fragrances to every living creature. Now stooping low, visiting the humblest flower, trying the temper of every leaf, tuning them, fondling and caressing them, stirring them in lusty exercise, carrying pollen from tree to tree, filling lakes with white lily spangles, chanting among pines, playing on every needle, on every mountain spire, on all the landscape as on a harp.

Trees

Happy the man to whom every tree is a friend — who loves them, sympathizes with them in their lives in mountain and plain, in their brave struggles on barren rocks and wind-swept ridges, and in joyous, triumphant exuberance in fertile ravines and valleys sheltered, waving their friendly branches, while we, fondling their shining plumage, rejoice with and feel the beauty and strength of their every attitude and gesture, the swirling surging of their lifeblood in every vein and cell. Great as they are and widespread their forests over the earth's continents and islands, we may love them all and carry them about with us in our hearts. And so with the smaller flower people that dwell beneath and around them, looking up with admiring faces, or down in thoughtful poise, making all the land or garden instinct with God.

Mountains

Nature's literature is written in mountain ranges along the sky, rising to heaven in triumphant songs in long ridge and dome and clustering peaks. When we dwell with mountains, see them face to face, every day, they seem as creatures with a sort of life — friends subject to moods, now talking, now taciturn, with whom we converse as man to man. They wear many spiritual robes, at times an aureole, something like the glory...the old painters put around the heads of saints....

The Mountains' Destiny

I often wonder what man will do with the mountains — that is, with their utilizable, destructible garments. Will he cut down all the trees to make ships and houses? If so, what will be the final and far upshot? Will human destructions like those of Nature — fire and flood and avalanche — work out a higher good, a finer beauty? Will a better civilization come in accord with obvious Nature, and all this wild beauty be set to human poetry and song? Another universal outpouring of lava, or the coming of a glacial period could scarce wipe out the flowers and shrubs more effectually than do the sheep. And what then is coming? What is the human part of the mountains' destiny?

Bears

Toiling in the treadmills of life we hide from the lessons of Nature. We gaze morbidly through civilized fog upon our beautiful world clad with seamless beauty, and see ferocious beasts and wastes and deserts. But savage deserts and beasts and storms are expressions of God's power inseparably companioned by love. Civilized man chokes his soul as the... Chinese their feet. We deprecate bears.

But grandly they blend with their native mountains. They roam the sandy slopes on lily meads, through polished glacier canyons, among the solemn firs and brown sequoia, manzanita, and chaparral, living upon red berries and gooseberries, little caring for rain or snow....Magnificent bears of the Sierra are worthy of their magnificent homes. They are not companions of men, but children of God, and His charity is broad enough for bears. They are the objects of His tender keeping....

There are no square-edged inflexible lines in nature. We seek to establish a narrow lane between ourselves and the feathery zeros we dare to call angels, but ask a partition barrier of infinite width to show the rest of creation its proper place.

Bears are made of the same dust as we, and breathe the same winds and drink of the same waters. A bear's days are warmed by the same sun, his dwellings are overdomed by the same blue sky, and his life turns and ebbs with heart-pulsings like ours, and was poured from the same First Fountain. And whether he at last goes to our stingy heaven or no, he has terrestrial immortality. His life not long, not short, knows no beginning, no ending. To him life unstinted, unplanned, is above the accidents of time, and his years, markless and boundless, equal Eternity.

Dawn

Morning comes again, hallowed with all the deeds of night. Here it is six or seven thousand feet above the sea, yet in all this tranquil scene we feel no remoteness, no rest from care and chafing duties because here they have no existence. Every sense is satisfied. For us there is no past, no future. We live in the present and are full. No room for hungry hopes, none for regrets, none for exultation, none for fear....

Breathing air: 1874

Every weary one seeking with damaged instinct the high founts of nature, when he chances into...the mountains, if accustomed to philosophize at all, if not too far gone in civilization, will ask, Whence comes? What is the secret of the mysterious enjoyment felt here — the strange calm, the divine frenzy? Whence comes the annihilation of bonds that seemed everlasting?...

Tell me what you will of the benefactions of city civilization, of the sweet security of streets — all as part of the natural upgrowth of man towards the high destiny we hear so much of. I know that our bodies were made to thrive only in pure air, and the scenes in which pure air is found. If the death exhalations that brood the broad towns in which we so fondly compact ourselves were made visible, we should flee as from a plague.

Go now and then for fresh life — if most of humanity must go through this town stage of development — just as divers hold their breath and come ever and anon to the surface to breathe....Go whether or not you have faith....Form parties, if you must be social, to go to the snow-flowers in winter, to the sun-flowers in summer....Anyway, go up and away for life; be fleet!

Bees

The common honeybees, gone wild in this sweet wilderness, gather tons of honey into the hollows of the trees and rocks, clambering eagerly through bramble and hucklebloom, shaking the clustered bells of the generous manzanita, now humming aloft among polleny willows and firs, now down on the ashy ground among small gilias and buttercups, and anon plunging into banks of snowy cherry and buckthorn....Besides the common honey-bee there are many others here, fine, burly, mossy fellows, such as were nourished on the mountains many a flowerly century before the advent of the domestic species — bumble-bees, mason bees, carpenter bees, and leaf cutters. Butterflies, too, and moths of every size and pattern; some wide-winged like bats, flapping slowly and sailing in easy curves; others like small flying violets shaking about loosely in short zigzag flights close to the flowers, feasting in plenty night and day.

Spring

Quick-growing bloom days when sap flows fast like the swelling streams. Rising from the dead, the work of the year is pushed on with enthusiasm as if never done before, as if all God's glory depended upon it; inspiring every plant, bird, and stream to sing with youth's exuberance, painting flower petals, making leaf patterns, weaving a fresh roof — all symbols of eternal love.

Water Music

When in making our way through a forest we hear the loud boom of a waterfall, we know that the stream is descending a precipice. If a heavy rumble and roar, then we know it is passing over a craggy incline. But not only are the existence and size of these larger characters of its channel proclaimed, but all the others. Go to the fountain-canyons of the Merced. Some portions of its channel will appear smooth, others rough, here a slope, there a vertical wall, here a sandy meadow, there a lake-bowl, and the young river speaks and sings all the smaller characters of the smooth slope and downy hush of meadow as faithfully as it sings the great precipices and rapid inclines, so that anyone who has learned the language of running water will see its character in the dark.

Beside the grand history of the glaciers and their own, the mountain streams sing the history of every avalanche or earthquake and of snow, all easily recognized by the human ear, and every word evoked by the falling leaf and drinking deer, beside a thousand other facts so small and spoken by the stream in so low a voice the human ear cannot hear them. Thus every event is written and spoken. The wing scars the sky, making a path inevitably as the deer in snow, and the winds all know it and tell it though we hear it not.

Gift

Bird song in the rain.... Delicious balmy, flower-opening rain, bathing and laving the great granite brows as gently as if refreshing a summer garden. Drip, drip down through the live oak groves and honeysuckle tangles of Sunnyside. A fragrant steam foretells the coming of a thousand flowers. Winter-hidden beetles and chrysalids and worms respond drowsily to the call of the warm rain's reviving touch. Fern coils grow in every cell; all the life of Sunnyside, rejoicing, tingles with the gift of the mountain clouds.

Summer

Here summer seems to be content, full of ripe beauty and joy. Young birds are tasting life in every grove. Happy myriads of flying insects shake all the air into music. Hundreds of flowers have ripened and planted their seeds, and all seem ready for the sere and yellow leaf. But the end is not yet, for remaining segments of sunny June are developing a glory that excelleth — a glory seldom seen by mortal eyes. The deep dense banks of green grow yet deeper and denser. The frost-nipped brackens call up their reserves, that soon overtop the tallest man and form a perfect forest of fronds that high overarch and embower groves of tall leaning grasses, and many with feathery dainty spikelets arise and bloom in the commonest places. Whole kingdoms of Ceanothus rise high above sedges and ferns like yellow stars on a green sky.

Spikes of purple mints eight feet in height shoot high above the common green. Family groups of starry Compositae glow on the meadow, and every other feature of plant beauty joins in the late summer glory.

Summer Storm

After the first hearty dash of rain, there is a lull of perfect stillness while the clouds crawl slowly in a squirming manner as if getting ready for steady work. At length the calm is broken by lightning that seems to strike midway between Glacier Point and the Royal Arches. This first stroke is followed by two others with long rolling billows of sound that beat on the massive walls in oft-repeated echoes. Then down comes the gentle rain, falling steadily all day. Fog-masses formed by the mixing of colder with warmer air creep here and there, while the outlines of the great headlands of the walls up and down the valley are softened and loom immensely higher in the gray misty atmosphere.

Everything Is Poetry

A bird is not feathers of certain colors, or members of a certain length — toes, claws, bill, gape, culmen — and of group so and so. This is not the bird that at heaven's gate sings, any more than man is a vertical vertebrate, five and one half feet long, with so many teeth and bones forming a right angle with the ground, though even all this is good in its way. On the rim of the Yosemite I once heard a man say: "How was this tremendous old rocky gorge formed?" "Oh, stop your science," said another of the party. "Hush! stand still and behold the glory of God!"

I suppose silent wonder would have been better, more natural at first. Still, as the warmth and beauty of fire are more enjoyed by those who, knowing something of the origin of wood and coal, see the dancing flames and are able to contemplate the grand show as having come from the sun ages ago, and slowly garnered in cells, so also are those Yosemite temples the more enjoyed by those who have traced, however dimly, the working of the Divine Mind in their making, who know why domes are here, and how sheer precipitous walls like El Capitan were predetermined by the crystallization of the granite in the dark, thousands of centuries before development, and who know how in the fullness of time the sun was called to lift water out of the sea in vapor which was carried by the winds to the mountains, crystallized into snow among the clouds, to fall on the summits, form glaciers, and bring Yosemite Valley and all the other Sierra features to the light. In offering us such vistas, thereby increasing our pleasure and admiration, science is divine!

Tuolumne Canyon

The Tuolumne Canyon is a street of the sublime Sierra City more than twenty miles long. Its rocks, one to five thousand feet high, present themselves on either side, like works of art elaborately sculptured, many places polished on which the sun glances as upon windows of glass. Here are all kinds of architecture, gables high and low, cornice and cusp, windows and arched entrances adorned with plants. Through the canyon flows a river clear as crystal, bordered with trees, Cassiope, fairest of shrubs, and sunny meadows here and there. Nature's best gardens are here in deepest repose, fountains of wild ever-playing water falling in every form — the endless song of Creation shaking the devout listener into newness of life. He who enters will hear a music which will never cease to vibrate in his life throughout all its blurring moil and toil, and to the beauties of this Tuolumne Street he will fain recur with fond memories, and all his material gains will rise in the balance against the riches garnered in her clear and rocky wilds.

Birds

Now a wide-winged hawk heaves in sight—
sailor of the air, fish of the upper sea, with
pectoral fins ten times as big as his body—
so high you scarce hear his fearless scream.

Now comes a cloud of cranes with loud up-
roar—"coor-r-r, coor-r-r"—breaking the crisp
air into greater waves with their voices than
with their broad brown wings, their necks
outstretched as if eager to see farther and go
faster, their legs folded and projecting back
like the handle of an umbrella. Looking down
as they go, they see the woods below dappled
with meadows and glistening with streams,
and know the location of all the frog bogs for
hundreds of miles.

A little dusky-crested bird dwells among
the willows, keeping the twigs in tremor,
though seldom seen. Now a linnet flits across
the open and lights on willow sprays, making
shimmer of shining leaves like the beautiful
disturbance made by ducks splashing down
from the sky into a sunny mirror-lake.

Jays with guttural notes hop from limb to
limb, leaving stiff dead twigs in fine vibration
like the fibers of a violin.

Woodpecker is drumming on hollow logs,

tapping dead spars. Then comes the way-cup with golden wings colored like October leaves, clad in perpetual autumn, the dearest of the woodpeckers, elegant in form notwithstanding his short barbed tail. He moves gracefully on the ground and sits well on slender sprays, and climbs as easily and fast as any of his tribe.

Now we hear the loud cackle and chuckle of the logcock, prince of Sierra woodpeckers, larger than a pigeon, with ivory bill, crimson head and jet wings, making the woods ring, loving the deepest dells where the sugar pine and sequoia grow tallest and cast dim shadows. Astonishing how far they are heard in calm weather drumming on dead sequoia tops.

Now a hummingbird as big as a bee alights wing-weary on a twig, and begins to smooth his feathers. He has flown many a mile since early morning, and touched more flowers than the botanist could gather in a week....

The Aurora Borealis

The most glorious of all the white night lights I ever beheld....Radiant glory of that midnight sky, as if the foundations were being laid for some fairer world. Beams of light in subdued splendor without effort, each shining shaft hasting in strong joy to its appointed place. Let there be light, and light was! Resplendent star-atoms shining, stars beyond stars....

Heaven and earth are one —
part of the vesture of God,
Around all the earth the deep Heaven lies and is
part of it.
The dark bodeful night
Becomes divine and glows transfigured in light,
Puts on the garment of Eternity
That comes from no earthly sun — a sight to be
worshipped.

Deer

Last night I slept under a grand old experienced juniper that had been nearly overthrown by a snow avalanche from the mountain dome above, but after coming down on his elbow, maintained his ground and grew and prospered, though never erect again. A grand tangle of branches and all kinds of recesses were about his roots. I cleared away stones and built up a wall to keep from rolling over a precipice of two hundred feet. An arm of the tree also held me. Just below my tree was a smaller one with protecting branches. On the very brink of the wall beneath is a deer's bed, a most complete concealment and resting-place and lookout. An hour or so before dark, I heard a sharp, loud snorting and, looking down into the valley spread maplike, I soon discovered a doe. She bounded up the mountainside where bushes and a gentle slope made it possible, often stopping to look back at me. Meanwhile I sat perfectly motionless. My brown shirt was like the junipers, and evidently she lost sight of me. After long and most perfect caution and deliberation she turned and moved slowly towards me, stopping constantly to look and smell. Her movements as she ran down the mountain-side, over logs, over rocks, over all kinds of brush, were most admirable, never straining although making enormous leaps. After coming within sixty or seventy yards of where I sat, she sniffed eagerly like a dog, turning up her head and trying different directions, then, catching my scent, she bounded off suddenly, snorting loud and quick until out of sight round the edge of a small fir grove. Soon she came on again with the same caution, again caught my scent, and again bounded away. This she repeated four or five times, after which I ceased to watch her. I think her fawns were hidden away in the chaparral. It is always to such wild and unfrequented canyons that they go for the purpose of rearing their young. I have often seen their beds while forcing my way over and under the most impenetrable jungles of ceanothus. manzanita, and chinquapin. This morning I saw two fawns groping their way down the mountain, called by their mother.

While I sat watching the deer as she bounded and snorted, a squirrel, evidently excited by the noise, came out and climbed a big boulder beneath me, and looked on at her performances as patiently and attentively as myself. Still nearer to me a fussy chipmunk, too heedless for such affairs, busied himself about a dainty supper which he obtained in a thicket of shadbushes whose fruit was ripe.

Indian Summer

Ambrosial days of thick gold. Crimson yellow of clouds. Small isles of mist transfigured. Water moving in luxurious languor, thick-swelling, rolling folds gliding in silence....

Sunlight lying thick and rich, brooding calm in the groves of pine down the rugged ice-carved canyon.

Bars of crimson at sunset, glorifying the edge of night.

Long after the valley lies quiet in shadow the domes still sing warmly with sunshine and echo it back to the meadows.

At night the great walls, unrelieved by any alternations of light and shadow, loom in un-broken masses to the stars.

The green pines far above wave and sing to the touch of the grand old winds.

Nowhere is God's love coined into more beautiful forms. Everywhere is timelessness and infinite leisure.

Life for Every Death

There need be no lasting sorrow for the death of any of Nature's creations, because for every death there is always born a corresponding life. And what life shall follow the death of the glacier, what creation shall come to that sea bottom on whose cold burnished rocks not a moss or dulse ever grew! In smooth hollows crystal lakes will live, to sandy beds sedges will come. Pines and firs will feather the moraines, advancing like an army and followed by the dearest flowers and happy animals, and instead of a robe of white ice will be a robe of yellow light upon the new Edens of the Sierra!

Sunset in Alaska

The most extravagantly beautiful of all the richly colored sunsets I have seen in this cool moist northland was one painted on a late July day when we were about halfway between Nanaimo and Fort Wrangell in the midst of one of the thickly sown archipelagoes. The most of the day had been rainy, but during the latter part of the afternoon the clouds cleared away — all save a few that lay along the horizon like islands in overlapping bars and belts, and in misty rolls on the mountains and down in some of the larger canyons of the mainland. It was a calm evening, a calmness that felt its way pervadingly back into one's soul, and the color came on gradually, increasing in extent of area and richness of tone (like a bank of roses coming into bloom in slow devices as if taking long to ripen); then it faded in the same way, though there was a marked dying-out of the more glowing fires at the moment of sunset. At a height of about thirty degrees, there was a heavy bank of cloud with dark gray sky above it, and its lower edge deeply tinged with red; below this were three horizontal bars of purple edged with gold, and pale yellow-green sky between them; while a spreading fan of flame radiated upward across these bars of color, fading on the edge of the separating radii in dull, lurid red. But beautiful and impressive as was this painting on the sky, the most novel and exciting effect was found in the atmosphere itself, which was so loaded with moisture that it was painted, or rather became, one mass of color, a thin translucent haze of wine purple, in which the islands seemed to float in a half-dissolved condition. A narrow strip of water, also red, seemed drawn like a border to the isles of the blessed. Luminous rolls of mist lay in the troughs between the mountains. Snowfields, glaciers, peaks were not simply steeped in the rosy atmosphere, but dissolved in purple flame. The main effect was seen in looking directly into the heart of the sunset as a focus. The three gold and purple bars, with yellow-green sky between; a dark cloud-bank overhead with heavy, lurid caves; then the whole mass of the air a soft, purple mist, with innumerable purple islands seen more and more faintly beyond and beyond, formed a vision of the isles of the blessed, spiritualized in faint, or rather, tender lines, dissolving yet distinct, more glorious in reality than ever the heart of poet conceived, a realization of a more extravagant dreamland than the poets of any nation have ever dared to write.

Lakes

Their shores curve in and out in bay and promontory, giving the appearance of lakes. The banks are overhung with wild rose and azalea and sedge and grass, and above these in beautiful combinations and in the glory of autumn colors are willows and alders, dogwood and balm of Gilead, a full blaze of yellow sunshine above, cool shadows beneath, with only flecks of sunlight on the bottom. The strained light filtering through painted leaves, as through colored windows, produces a dreamy enchanted atmosphere like that of some old cathedral. The banks of moss and liverwort and tinted ferns that overlean the placid water are reflected with charming effect, colored light from above falling on colored leaves, sifting through and falling on the brown pebbles of the bottom of the pool, then partly reflected back into the bright foliage. The surface of the pool is stirred gently in some spots by bands of water beetles, or the swimming strokes of spiders and dipping of dragonflies. Now and then a trout shoots from shelter to shelter beneath fallen logs.

The noonday enchantment of these pools is entirely unlike any other effect, and must be experienced to be known. No wind stirs. The falls too are quiet, slipping down the grand precipices in lacework, with scarce a sound, silently as sunbeams. The whole valley floor is a finely blended mosaic of greens and purples, yellows and reds. Everything is passive in appearance, even the unflinching rocks seem strangely soft in beauty of lines with their strength hidden and held in abeyance.

Survival

The beauty and completeness of a wild apple tree living its own life in the woods is heartily acknowledged by all those who have been so happy as to form its acquaintance. The fine wild piquancy of its fruit is unrivaled, but in the great question of quantity as human food, wild apples are found wanting. Man, therefore, takes the tree from the woods, manures and prunes and grafts, plans and guesses, adds a little of this and that, selects and rejects, until apples of every conceivable size and softness are produced, like nutgalls in response to the irritating punctures of insects. Orchard apples are to me the most eloquent words that culture has ever spoken, but they reflect no imperfection upon Nature's spicy crab. Every cultivated apple is a crab, not improved, *but cooked,* variously softened and swelled out in the process, mellowed, sweetened, spiced, and rendered pulpy and foodful, but as utterly unfit for the uses of Nature as a meadowlark killed and plucked and roasted. Give to Nature every cultured apple — codling, pippin, russet — and every sheep so laboriously compounded — muffled Southdowns, hairy Cotswolds, wrinkled Merinos — and she would throw the one to her caterpillars, the other to her wolves.

Night Thoughts

When the day is done, the bough bed made, bread eaten, the fire glows cheerily in the majestic depths of darkness, giving back the sunshine gathered from the sifting sunbeams of a hundred summers, gathered in cells like honey, illumining the flowers in the grove or the one tree, the arching grass tuft, the daisy. How living they look — like fairy spirits clad in forms woven from sunbeams! What expression in their faces, and as we lie dressed, how profound the calm, and how profound the action! We hear the heartbeats of Nature, the tides of the life sap in every cell, the swirling, eddying currents. The river song is louder, filling all the canyon. The fall nearest, how much louder, more impressive the roar, and how much firmer the low tones and wider the range! How many birds and beasts are awake and waiting; how many feet and wings are active, eyes shining like stars! The bear and the deer and the mice, marmots, moles, and gophers — a curious sturdy race living always in the dark, to whom the daisy-starred sod is a sky. And as we lie, our face to the heavens, the stars how they shine! As we gaze, they call us into the far regions of thought, singing the song of Creation's dawn. From the bottom of a canyon where I lie alone, I hear that song the best, as the constellations swing into view over the rim of the rocks, the same stars the shepherds looked at on the plains, thousands of years ago. How many tubes are pointed at them even tonight. Mills of God, every one of them grinding out gusts of light, sending a blessing to each living creature in the sea, on the land, in every nook and corner, the height and depth of the round globe itself. On this shining spark in the firmament every crystal is throbbing, sleeping, yet waking —

the quartz, mica, feldspar, tourmaline, hornblende, garnet. What a picture of celestial industry is beheld in the heavens! What a storm of harmonious motion, enduring forever, abating never!

The Earthquake

It was a calm moonlit night, and no sound was heard for the first minute or two save a low muffled underground rumbling and a slight rustling of the agitated trees, as if, in wrestling with the mountains, Nature were holding her breath. Then, suddenly, out of the strange silence and strange motion there came a tremendous roar. The Eagle Rock, a short distance up the valley, had given way, and I saw it falling in thousands of the great boulders I had been studying so long, pouring to the valley floor in a free curve luminous from friction, making a terribly sublime and beautiful spectacle — an arc of fire fifteen hundred feet span, as true in form and as steady as a rainbow, in the midst of the stupendous roaring rock storm. The sound was inconceivably deep and broad and earnest, as if the whole earth, like a living creature, had at last found a voice and were calling to her sister planets....

Nature, usually so deliberate in her operations, then created, as we have seen, a new set of features, simply by giving the mountains a shake — changing not only the high peaks and cliffs, but the streams. As soon as these rock avalanches fell, every stream began to sing new songs; for in many places thousands of boulders were hurled into their channels, roughening and half damming them, compelling the waters to surge and roar in rapids where before they were gliding smoothly. Some of the streams were completely dammed, driftwood, leaves, etc., filling the interstices between the boulders, thus giving rise to lakes and level reaches; and these, again, after being gradually filled in, to smooth meadows, through which the streams now silently meander; while at the same time some of the taluses took the places of old meadows and groves. Thus rough places were made smooth, and smooth places rough. But on the whole, by what...seemed pure confusion and ruin, the landscapes were enriched....

All Nature's wildness tells the same story. Storms of every sort, torrents, earthquakes, cataclysms, "convulsions of nature," etc., how-

ever mysterious and lawless at first sight ...
are only harmonious notes in the song of creation, varied expressions of God's love.

The Dog Stickeen

Muir, like Thoreau, found companionship, joy and an
education in his dealings with animals. His dog Stick-
een, "an Indian cur" as Muir called him, shared many
wilderness adventures with him.

A good-natured sailor and vagabond, he was
fond of wandering but without visible enthusiasm, nosing among logs and trees with
sober, unhasting industry, now and then shaking the rain from his hair or the dew from
the huckleberry bushes, heeding no kind of
weather, never in a hurry or fuss, eating as
if it were a sad duty.

He was smooth and glossy as a berry. His
little round feet made no sound on the moss
carpet of the woods, turf and moss, nor on
the glacier that never before felt the foot of
man or dog.
No mark of years was on him — he seemed
neither old nor young. He always looked grave,

no matter how playful you might be with him; scratch his ears, pat his head, set him up on hind legs, or cuddle him on your lap, he was still irresistibly grave — not a tail-wag. A little black horizontal philosopher, calm, pensive, silently watchful....

This poor little wild apostle of Alaska, child-dog of the wilderness, taught me much. Anyhow, we were nearly killed and we both learned a lesson never to be forgotten, and are the better man and dog for it — learned that human love and animal love, hope and fear, are essentially the same, derived from the same source and fall on all alike like sunshine.

He enlarged my life, extended its boundaries. I always befriended animals and have said many a good word for them. Even to the least-loved mosquitoes I gave many a meal, and told them to go in peace.

In all my wild walks, seldom have I had a more definite and useful message to bring back. Stickeen was the herald of a new gospel.... And it as in that dreadful crevasse that I tried so hard to avoid that I saw through him down into the depths of our common nature.

Any glimpse into the life of an animal quickens our own and makes it so much the larger and better every way. But this was more than a glimpse, it was a deep look "ben in the heart," as the Scotch say, and made all animals friends and fellow-mortals indeed.

Stickeen's homely clay was instinct with celestial fire, had in it a little of everything that is in man; he was a horizontal man-child, his heart beating in accord with the universal heart of Nature. He had his share of hopes, fears, joys, griefs, imagination, memory, soul as well as body — and surely a share of that immortality which cheers the best saint that ever walked on end....

Following a storm, in an area of icy cliffs and canyons, Stickeen gets stranded, and is left alone on the side of that awful abyss, unspeakably lonely, so pitifully helpless and small, overshadowed with darkness and the dread of death....

But in his little hairy body there was a strong heart, for notwithstanding his piercing recognition of deadly danger, he was able to hush his screaming fears and make firm his trembling limbs.

At length, as with the hushed, breathless courage of despair, he slipped down into the shadow of death, the storm was not heard or seen by either of us. I saw only those pathetic, feeble little feet as he slid them over the round bank into the first step. Soon the hind pair followed, and all four were bunched in it. Then he worked them down into the next notch, and the next, and, hushed and silent, lifted his feet slowly in exact measure; I, breathlessly watching him walk along the long narrow sliver, waited on my knees ready to help him up the cliff at the end; but when he reached it, he hooked his feet into the steps of the ice-ladder, and bounded past me in a rush. Then such a revulsion from fear to joy! Such a gush of canine hallelujahs burst forth on the safe side of the gulf of ice!

How eloquent he became, though so generally taciturn — a perfect poet of misery, and triumphant joy! He rushed round and round in crazy whirls of joy, rolled over and over, bounded against my face, shrieked and yelled as if trying to say, "Saved, saved, saved!"

…And so, the Lord loving us both, we got back to camp. He was indeed a fellow-creature — a little boy in distress in guise of a dog.

"A Mysterious Presence"

Gain health from lusty, heroic exercise, from free, firm-nerved adventures without anxiety in them, with rhythmic leg motion in runs over boulders requiring quick decision for every step. Fording streams, tingling with flesh brushes as we slide down white slopes thatched with close snow-pressed chaparral, half swimming or flying or slipping — all these make good counterirritants. Then enjoy the utter peace and solemnity of the trees and stars. Find many a plant and bird living sequestered in hollows and dells — little chambers in the hills. Feel a mysterious presence in a thousand coy hiding things.

Go free as the wind, living as true to Nature as those gray and buff people of the sequoias and the pines.

Winter Landscape

The Lyell group of mountains show their peaks striking sharply into the dark sky with streaks of foamlike waves. Irised clouds hover above them, and here and there a cloud caught on a peak trails horizontally like a banner. The shadows of the peaks lie clearly outlined on the ample sheets of snow below that, like drapery, conform to the rugged anatomy of the landscape. Beneath the snowfields one sees the forests dark by contrast.

In front of all this grand picture of mountain and forest are laid the massive, snowless gray walls of the valley, swooping majestically to the bottom and planting their feet firmly among pine groves and meadows. The river glows like a mirror, and in every rapid the sun is sowing spangles. The meadows are lovely in color — yellow with sedge, and brown with patches of fern. The sun glowing on smooth bosses, and groves of erect taper pines with their shadows produce light and shade among the rocks.

The winds sing on among the pines and firs. Jays scream lustily. The snow is melting into music. There is scarce any frost at night. Little wrens and mouselike chickadees appear in considerable numbers.

Clouds' Rest is nearly solid white. Tissiack is white on her crown, and white-streaked and dusted in her many folds of rock clothing. Starr King has a dense black forest of fir sweeping up his slopes from the north. The top of his cone is white on the north, gray on the south.

Shadows from Glacier Point as a center sweep up the valley, shearing off the glow from river and meadow.

All the fields of God, whether reposing in the garments of winter or of summer, sing of gentleness and love.

Eventide

For a while not a sound. Then the creak of myriad voices fills the night with soothing, slumberous stir — all one subdued tone. Yet above the general level of sound, like ripples on a woodland lake, a few notes are heard — tiny cricketlike musical creaks and chirps, infinitely sweet.

The woodpecker is latest at work, not like the hasty laborer stopping before his task is done....

Beetles drone and boom, then drop into silence. Bats, winging on easy whirls, circle in bays and deep pools of air among the trees.

A meteor flashes athwart the sky, startling us into a sense of the majestic movements of other worlds. Stars, though bright, are far less brilliant than on the heights.

Ant lions flutter in campfire light. And, circling round, the grand tree shafts are seen, the eye being confined to a few, not roaming loosely over all the woods....A soft, plaintive note like that of a bird is heard frequently, but I have not yet traced it to its source.... Then the owl unmistakable, and how cheery!

Stars glow brighter, for the moon is still below the horizon. Here and there one is seen among the branches, like a white incense lily; or past the black boles, alone over the hills.

Mayhap one's mind will wander to other woods where the sun still shines. But that is not our affair, and if quite healthy, we shall be full of our own night.

John Muir: Milestones

1838	Born in Dunbar, Scotland, April 21.
1849	Emigrated with family to Wisconsin frontier.
1860	Won prize for inventions at State Agricultural Fair. Entered University of Wisconsin.
1867	Walked from Kentucky to Florida. Wrote first journal.
1868	Arrived in California, March 28.
1869-73	Made headquarters in Yosemite Valley. Explored Sierra for evidence of glacial action.
1874-76	Ascended Mount Shasta. Began intensive study of trees. Launched movement for federal control of forests.
1879	First trip to Alaska.
1880	Married Louie Wanda Strentzel, April.
1882-87	Returned home to raise fruit.
1889	Worked for the creation of the Yosemite National Park.
1891-92	Founded Sierra Club.
1893-94	Visited Europe.
1896-98	Received M.A. from Harvard. Worked with National Forest Commission. Received LL.D. from University of Wisconsin.
1901-02	Began fight to save the Hetch Hetchy Valley.
1903-04	Guided President Roosevelt through the Yosemite. Made world tour.
1906	Explored Arizona.
1913	Lost fight to save Hetch Hetchy Valley.
1914	Died in Los Angeles, December 24.

Set in Vladimir, a Roman typeface
designed by Vladimir Andrich
for the Alphatype Corporation.
Printed on Crown Royale Book paper.
Designed by Jay Johnson.